Learn About
Food

BRIMAX

What is food?

Food is what keeps us healthy and strong. Eating food regularly provides us with five important nutrients – proteins, fats, vitamins, carbohydrates and minerals. It also gives us some of the water that is essential for the body to function properly.

Food gives us energy. It is the fuel our body needs to stay alive. If we did not eat and drink, we wouldn't be able to...

jump

play

run

sing

or grow!

Where does food come from?

All over the world, thousands of people are busy...

planting

growing

harvesting

**and preparing
food to eat.**

Most of us buy our food in shops and markets.

We then cook it...

and eat it!

Meat and fish

Meat comes from different kinds of animals.

Most people cook meat before they eat it.

Pork, ham and bacon come from pigs.

Beef comes from cows.

Mutton and lamb come from sheep.

Chickens and turkeys are raised mostly on farms. We call this type of meat 'poultry'.

Fish and shellfish come from rivers and the sea.

Fruit and vegetables

Fruit and vegetables help to provide us with the vitamins and natural sugars our bodies need to stay healthy and strong. Some vegetables, such as potatoes, supply carbohydrates for energy.

Fruit grows on bushes and trees.

It can be eaten raw...

...cooked in pies, or served as a delicious hot dessert on its own.

Many fruits are made into juices and jam or jelly.

Salad is eaten raw,

but most vegetables
are cooked and
often served with
meat or fish.

Some vegetables, like potatoes and carrots, grow beneath the ground.

Other vegetables, like cabbages and peas, grow above the ground.

Food that is good for you

Your body must have the right type of food to stay healthy.
That means eating a variety of different foods each day.

**Meat and poultry
provide protein.**

**Fish and shellfish are rich
in body-building protein,
minerals and vitamins.**

Bread, rice and pasta are staple, or basic, foods that provide bulk, energy and protein.

Food keeps us warm, gives us energy and helps us grow. Our daily pattern of eating and drinking is called our diet.

Some people, called vegetarians, choose to not eat meat. To make up for this, they eat extra portions of vegetables, grains, cereals and legumes, such as peas and beans.

Without the proper food, you wouldn't have the energy to run or play!

Protein comes mainly from meat, fish, milk, eggs, nuts and cereals. Milk and cheese contain lots of calcium and help make your bones and teeth strong.

Don't forget, water is very important, too!

A balanced diet

Eating too much or too little food is very bad for you.

You must eat a balanced diet with plenty of good things like fresh fruit and salad every day!

Too many sweet foods and sugary drinks are bad for your teeth. Your dentist may find a hole in a tooth that will need a filling.

Not eating enough vitamins and minerals can make you feel tired, weak and ill.

Some people can get sick if they eat certain foods, such as nuts or shellfish.

This is because they are allergic to these foods.

Special food

People eat special kinds of food to celebrate different festivals.

At Easter, people in some countries eat chocolate eggs.

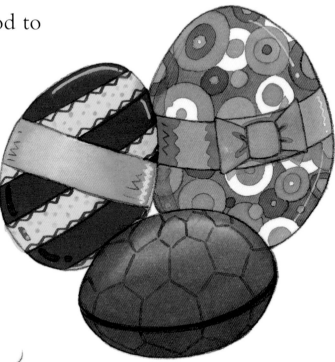

In the USA, people eat roast turkey to celebrate Thanksgiving. In the UK, people often eat roast turkey to celebrate Christmas.

Availability of food varies across the world depending on climate, local customs and religious beliefs. The diet of some Aboriginal Australians and Africans includes insects and grubs! That might sound strange, but in countries where food is in short supply, insects and grubs are a great source of energy.

Shrove Tuesday, or 'Mardi gras', is celebrated in many countries by eating pancakes.

Famous food

Some countries are known for producing certain foods, many of which have become very popular all over the world.

Hamburgers come from the USA.

Curry comes from Asia. Curries can be very hot and spicy. But some are quite mild.

Pasta comes from Italy, where it is cooked and served with delicious sauces.

Pizza also comes from Italy. It is served with different toppings, such as tomatoes, peppers, meat - and cheese, of course!

Mixing food

Some foods can be mixed together and cooked to make all sorts of different and delicious foods.

Cows produce milk...

from which we make cheese and butter.

Wheat and corn are ground into flour to make bread.

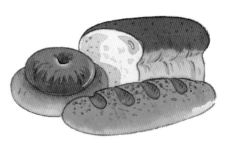

You can mix

sugar,

flour,

eggs,

butter,

and milk,

to make a lovely cake.

Mixing the right foods gives us a balanced diet.